The aim of this revision Guide is to give you an overview of all the topics in the Year 12 economics specification exam. The guide is a summary so do not use it as your only revision source.

AQA – 7135
Cambridge – 9708
Edexcel – 8ECO
OCR - H060

Contents

Microeconomics

Macroeconomics

Chapter 1 Introduction to Economics

Definitions
The Basic Economic Problem - there are limited resources but wants are infinite, this means that choices have to be made.

Scarce resources - those which are not unlimited in supply e.g. oil.

Non- renewable resources - resources which will eventually run out e.g. oil and coal.

Renewable resources - resources which can regenerate e.g. wind and solar energy.

Free good - a good which does not cost anything e.g. air and sea water NB free samples are not free goods because they cost the supplier.

Economic good - a good which has a cost e.g. coffee and biscuits.

A positive economic statement - objective statements which can be tested eg a reduction in the price of ice cream will increase the demand.

A normative statement - an opinion / value judgement e.g. more should be spent on the NHS.

Ceteris Paribus - 'all other things are equal'. When testing economic theory we only change one thing at a time to assess the impact of that change.

Opportunity cost - the benefit of the next best alternative forgone eg if the government spends more on schools they have less to spend on the NHS.

The Key Economic Decisions
What to produce? How to produce? and for whom to produce?

Factors of Production
Land - this is the space as well as the natural resources in it and on it.
Eg minerals, sea water, car park, area where the firm is built.

Labour - the workers e.g. chefs, cleaners.
Quality of workers i.e. skills is important as well as the quantity. A country with a large unskilled labour force will have lower growth.

Capital - man made resources such as machinery, factories and equipment used to produce goods and services.
Spending more on capital goods will help a business grow.

Enterprise - the factor which brings together the other factors of production and takes risks in order to make a profit.

Rewards to the factors of production
Land - rent
Labour - wages
Capital - interest
Enterprise - profit

Economic Agents
Producers - firms which produce goods and services.
Goals - maximise profit; maximise sales; maximise revenue; ethical objectives.
Consumers - people who buy the goods and services.
Goals - maximise utility/ satisfaction, maximise wages.
Governments - set the rules and produce some goods and services.
Goals - maximise welfare of the citizens; economic growth; low inflation; full employment; equilibrium in the balance of payments.

The Margin
Marginal refers to change/additional.
Marginal cost - additional cost of producing one more unit.
Marginal revenue - additional revenue from selling one more unit.
Marginal utility - additional benefit from consuming one more unit.
Marginal product - additional output from employing one more worker.

Diminishing marginal utility - the additional utility (satisfaction) from consuming one more unit declines e.g. first packet of crisps gives a lot of satisfaction, the next not quite as much.

How Consumers Act Rationally

Traditional economic theory assumes that consumers, producers and governments aim to maximise utility.

A rational consumer will consume where marginal utility = price. Eg if the first packet of crisps cost 60p and the consumer gains 80p satisfaction from it then this packet of crisps will be consumed. The utility from the second packet might be 70p, at a price of 60p the consumer will still consume this second packet. The third packet might give 50p worth of satisfaction but is costing 60p so this third packet will not be consumed.

Why consumers do not behave Rationally

- They may not have all the information they require about all their options.
- Information may be incorrect.
- There might be too much data to process.
- Calculating and processing the information is time consuming and might be difficult for some consumers e.g. when booking a holiday a consumer needs to know prices of hotel, flight, insurance, car parking, taxi, food. They might not have all of the information when comparing two holidays or some of the information might be out of date. Additionally, they might forget they need insurance.

Functions of the Price Mechanism

- **Rationing** - if there is high demand for a product but shortage of supply the price mechanism will ration out this demand by increasing price.
- **Incentive** - higher prices act as an incentive to firms to produce more as they are motivated by profits.
- **Signalling** - price increases act as a signal to producer that demand is high so they will produce more.

Chapter 2 Specialisation, Trade and Markets

Definitions

Free market economy - resources are allocated by supply and demand, there is limited government intervention. In a pure free market economy there would be no government intervention (this does not exist).

Command (planned) economy - the government decides how to allocate resources eg they tell firms what flavour crisps to produce and how many. North Korea is an example of a command economy.

Mixed economy - the government (public sector) and private sector produce goods and services. Most countries are mixed but some have more government intervention than others eg in the UK healthcare and education are provided by the government but in the US these are provided by the private sector.

Specialisation - where an individual, firm, region or economy focuses production on one good or narrow range of goods eg Apple specialises in technology; the UK specialises in financial services.

Division of labour - a type of specialisation where a worker focuses on one task e.g. on a car production line or a teacher specialising in teaching economics.

Barter - where goods are exchanged for goods rather than for money.

Productivity _–(AQA only)_   output per unit of input e.g. labour productivity is output per worker per hour or per day.

Advantages of a free market system
- Firms are incentivised to be efficient due to competition in the market.
- Enterprise is encouraged due to rewards in the form of high profit.
- Choice for consumers due to competition in the market.

Disadvantages of a Free Market System
- Monopolies may be present which exploit consumers.
- Income inequalities due to lack of support from the government.
- Some goods may not be produced due to lack of profit but they might be needed e.g. street lights.

Advantages of a Command Economy
- Low unemployment due to the government providing jobs.
- No monopolies due to government intervention.
- Welfare is maximised because government has control so can ensure certain goods are produced as well as redistribute income fairly.

Disadvantages of a Command Economy
- Less choice for consumers because firms are told what to produce so usually a limited range offered.
- Poor decision making by the government as they might not have all the information.
- Lower efficiency due to governments not having profit maximisation as an objective so not innovating or using new technology.

Advantages of Specialisation
- Firms/countries can focus on what they are best at or have the resources for.
- Higher quality and better products can be produced.
- Larger output due to focusing on a narrow range of goods means larger economies of scale so lower average costs.
- A reputation can be established.

Disadvantages of Specialisation
- Countries will not be self sufficient; a problem in times of war or trade disputes.
- A country may rely on raw materials which eventually run out.
- Transport costs may mean that there are no/ minimal benefits from trading.

Advantages of division of labour
- Workers can focus on the task they are best at so efficiency is improved.
- Workers may be more motivated as they are doing the job they enjoy/are best at.
- Less equipment will be needed if the worker is only doing one task.
- Less training required if the worker is only focusing on one task/small range of tasks.

Disadvantages of division of labour
- Workers may become bored/demotivated and make mistakes if they are working on a menial task on a production line.
- If one worker on a production line is slow/unwell all the stages after that worker get slowed down.
- Workers find it hard to get another job as they have a narrow range of skills.

Functions of Money
- Medium of exchange
- Store of value
- Measure of value
- Standard of deferred payment

Characteristics of Money
- Durable
- Divisible
- Portable
- Uniform
- Limited in supply
- Acceptable

This page is Edexcel only

Adam Smith (1723-1790)
- A big believer in the free market and invisible hand - resources allocated by market forces of supply and demand.
- There should be no monopolies dominating the market.
- There is a place for Government intervention.

Karl Marx (1818-1883)
- Profit maximising producers exploit workers by paying low wages.
- Production should be organised centrally.

Friedrich Hayek (1899-1992)
- Supporter of free market.
- Governments shouldn't intervene because they have insufficient information.

Chapter 3 Production Possibility Curves / Frontiers

Definitions
A production possibility frontier shows the maximum potential output of two goods when all resources are fully and efficiently employed.

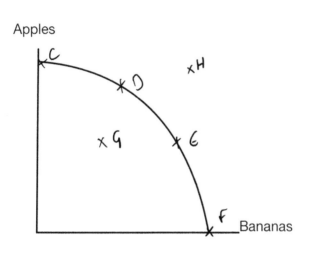

Points C,D,E and F are equally efficient

Point C shows only apples are produced

Point F shows only bananas are produced

Point G is inefficient / unemployed resources

Point H is unattainable with current resources

Shifts in the PPF

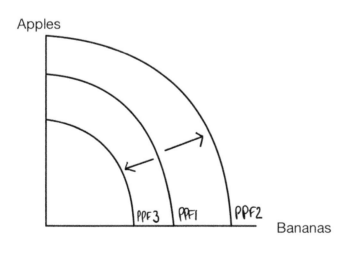

A shift outwards from PPF1 to PPF2 shows an increase in the maximum potential output/ economic growth

A shift inwards from PPF1 to PPF2 shows an decrease in the maximum potential output

Causes of a Shift Outwards
- Improvements in technology
- Increased amount of technology
- Education and training
- Increased immigration

Causes of a Shift Inwards
- War
- Natural disasters e.g. floods
- Increased emigration

Opportunity Cost and the PPF

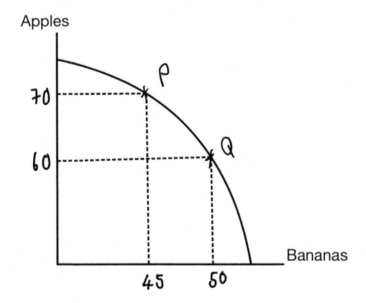

The opportunity cost of moving from P to Q is 10 apples

The opportunity cost of moving from Q to P is 5 bananas

Chapter 4 Demand and Supply

Definitions

Demand - the quantity consumers are willing and able to buy at a given price.

Individual demand - demand for a produce by an individual.

Market demand - demand for the product from all individuals added together.

Supply - the quantity that suppliers are willing and able to supply at a given price.

Individual supply - the supply by one individual firm

Market supply - the supply of a product by all firms added together.

Consumer surplus - the difference between the price consumers are prepared to pay and the price they actually pay.

Producer surplus - the difference between the price producers are prepared to accept and the price they receive.

Normal goods - as income increases demand increases e.g. clothes.

Inferior goods - as income increases demand decreases e.g. spam.

Giffen goods - as price increases demand increases. They are an inferior good which consumers cannot go without, so if they become more expensive consumers have to give up something else and will buy more of the inferior good to fill the gap e.g. bread or rice.

Joint demand/ complements - goods which are consumed together e.g. tea and biscuits.

Competitive demand/ substitutes - goods which are alternatives e.g. bounty and twix.

Composite demand - goods which have more than one use so are demanded in multiple markets e.g. wood is used to make tables and paper.

Derived demand - the demand for a good is due to the demand for another good e.g. the demand for wood is derived due to the demand for tables.

Joint supply - the production of one good automatically leads to the production of another good e.g. if the supply of lamb meat increases there will be more wool.

Competitive supply - where a good is used in the production of two or more products e.g. milk is used to produce cheese or yogurt.

The Demand Curve

A reduction in price leads to an increase in demand known as an extension in demand.

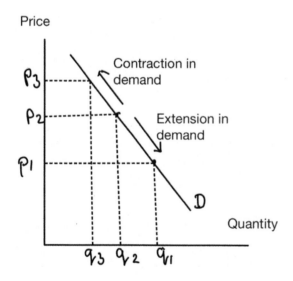

An increase in price leads to a decrease in demand - known as a contraction in demand.

Shifts in the Demand Curve to the Right

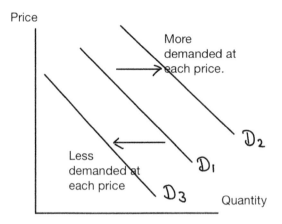

- An increase in income if the good is a normal good e.g. takeaways.
- A decrease in income for an inferior good e.g. spam.
- An increase in population/ an increase in the number of people in a certain age group e.g. an ageing population will mean more demand for bungalows.
- An increase in the price of a substitute e.g. if the price of bounty goes up the demand for twix will increase.
- A decrease in the price of a complement e.g. if the price of strawberries falls the demand for cream will increase.
- Changes in tastes and preferences e.g. advertising of the good or popularity of the good changes such as ice creams in the summer.

The Upward Sloping Demand Curve

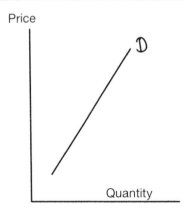

As price increases demand increases, this will be the case in a few circumstances:
- Giffen goods e.g. bread or rice
- Ostentatious goods e.g. designer clothes or certain high end cars
- Speculative goods e.g. shares and currency

Consumer surplus

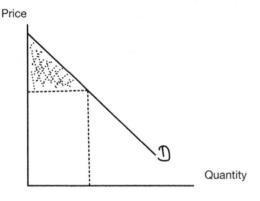

An increase in the price will lead to a decrease in consumer surplus.

The Supply Curve

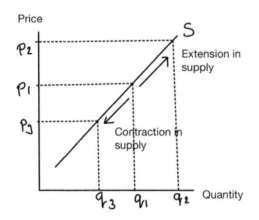

An increase in price means supplier are prepared to supply more due to the higher profit margin. There will be an extension in supply

A decrease in price will lead to a contraction in supply.

Shifts in the Supply Curve to the right

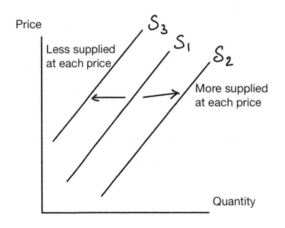

Lowering the costs of production will means suppliers are prepared to supply more at each price due to the higher profit.

- Lower price of raw materials
- Lower energy costs
- Improvements in technology
- Lower labour costs e.g. labour becomes more productive so cost per unit of output is lower
- Subsidies (taxes will shift supply to the left)

Producer Surplus

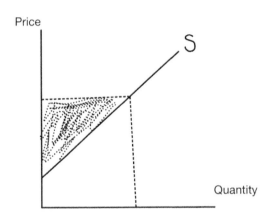

A fall in price will lead to a decrease in producer surplus.

Equilibrium Price

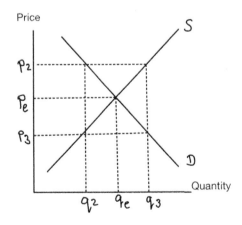

When price is P2 there will be excess supply of q3-q2. The price will fall to Pe to sell the excess supply.

When price is P3 there will be excess demand of q3-q2. The price will increase to Pe to ration out the shortage.

Changes in Equilibrium Price

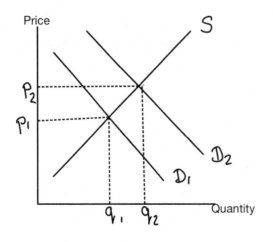

E.g. There is an increase in income

The demand curve for iPhones will shift to the right because they are a normal good. This will lead to an increase in price from P1 to P2 and an increase in quantity traded from q1 to q2. There will be an extension in supply.

E.g. The government gives a subsidy to farmers producing milk.
The supply curve for milk will shift to the right.
Price falls from P1 to P2, quantity traded increases from q1 to q2. There will be an extension in demand.

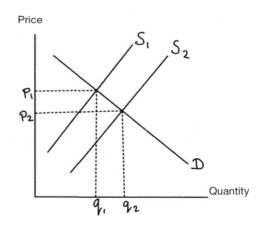

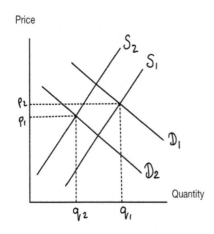

E.g. An increase in cost of cocoa and government campaigns to encourage people to eat healthier. The demand curve for chocolate will shift left due to change in tastes and preference. The supply curve will shift left due to increase in costs of production.
Price increase from P1 to P2, quantity traded falls from q1 to q2.

Chapter 5 Elasticity

Definitions and Equations

Price elasticity of demand (PED) - the responsiveness of quantity demanded due to a change in price.

PED = % change in quantity demanded / % change in price

Income elasticity of demand (YED) - the responsiveness of quantity demanded due to a change in income.

YED = % change in quantity demanded / % change in income

Cross elasticity of demand (XED) - the responsiveness of quantity demanded of good A due to a change in price of good B.

XED = % change in quantity demanded of good A / % change in price of good B

Price elasticity of supply (PES) - the responsiveness of quantity supplied due to a change in price.

PES = % change in quantity supplied / % change in price

Types of Elasticity

When price increases demand falls so PED will always be negative. When determining the type of elasticity the numerical value is considered, the negative sign is ignored e.g. if PED is -5 the good will have elastic demand because 5 is greater than 1.

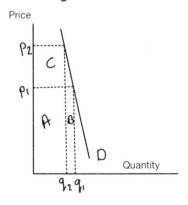

Inelastic demand PED < 1

When price is P1 total revenue = A + B
When price is P2 total revenue = A + C
Area C is bigger than area B so when price increases TR increases for goods with inelastic demand.

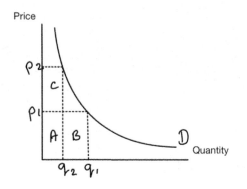

Elastic demand PED > 1

When price is P1 total revenue = A + B
When price is P2 total revenue = A + C
Area C is smaller than area B so when price increases TR decreases for goods with inelastic demand.

Unitary elastic demand PED = 1

When price is P1 total revenue = A + B
When price is P2 total revenue = A + C
Area B = Area C so TR stays the same when price increases

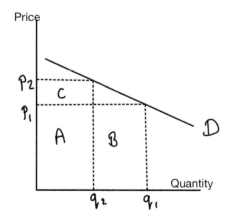

Extreme elasticities

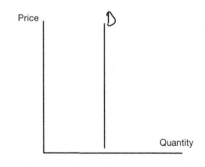

Perfectly inelastic demand PED = 0

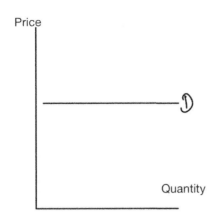

Perfectly elastic demand
PED = infinity

Factors Determining PED

1. **Number of substitutes** - if there are many substitutes a rise in price will mean consumers have alternatives to choose from so there will be a big reduction in demand i.e. demand will be elastic e.g. chocolate buttons.
2. **Proportion of income spent on the good** - if the good takes up a large proportion of a consumers income an increase in price will be significant so there will be a big reduction in demand i.e. demand will be elastic e.g. holidays.
3. **Luxury or necessity** - if the good is a necessity a rise in price will not have much impact on demand for the good i.e. demand will be inelastic e.g. toilet rolls
4. **Addiction** - if the consumer is addicted a rise in price will have little impact on demand i.e. demand will be inelastic e.g. cigarettes.
5. **Brand loyalty** - if consumers are loyal to a brand, when price increases they will not cut consumption by much i.e. demand will be inelastic e.g. Apple iPhone.
6. **Time** - in the short run consumers may not be able to switch to an alternative as it takes time to find a suitable substitute. In the short run demand will often be inelastic but in the long run more elastic.

Income Elasticity of Demand

Normal goods - positive YED e.g. mobile phones - as income goes up demand goes up.
Inferior goods - negative YED e.g. public transport - as income goes up demand goes down.

Income elastic - YED is greater than 1
Income inelastic - YED is less than 1

Cross Elasticity or Demand

Substitutes - positive XED e.g. whiskers and felix - as the price of whiskas goes up the demand for felix goes up.
Complements - negative XED e.g. cereals and milk - as the price of cereals goes up the demand for milk goes down as fewer cereals will be bought.

Price Elasticity of Supply
PES will always be positive - as price increases, suppliers wish to supply more

Inelastic supply
PES < 1

Hard to increase supply when price increases

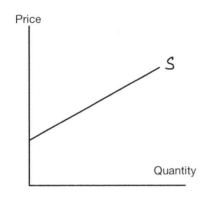

Elastic supply
PES > 1

Easy to increase supply when price increases

Unitary elastic supply
PES = 1

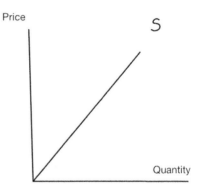

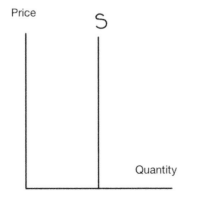

Perfectly inelastic supply
PES = 0

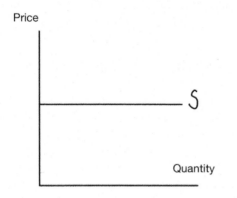

**Perfectly elastic supply
PES = infinity**

Factors Determining PES

1. **Stock levels** - if the firm has high levels of the product in storage it is easy to increase supply in response to a rise in price. Supply will be elastic. This tends to be the case with non perishable goods or goods which do not go out of fashion e.g. shampoo.
2. **Level of unemployment** - when unemployment is high it is easy to increase supply as it is easy to get more workers to produce more. Supply will be elastic.
3. **Time to grow/ produce** - goods which take a long time to grow will have inelastic supply as supply cannot be increased quickly e.g. apples.
4. **Time period** - in short run it may be hard for a firm to increase supply due to factors of production being fixed. Supply will be more inelastic in the short run. In the long run more machinery can be bought or they can move to a bigger factory.

Chapter 6 Market Failure

Definitions

Market failure - the free market fails to allocate resources efficiently e.g. there are shortages or externalities are ignored.

Positive externality/external benefit - benefit to a 3rd party e.g. when someone has flowers in their garden other people benefit from this.

Negative externality/external cost - cost to a 3rd party e.g. noise from building works.

Social cost - private cost + external cost.

Social benefit - private benefit + external benefit.

Merit goods - goods which are have benefits to society as well as individuals AND consumers often underestimate the benefits e.g. vaccinations.

Demerit goods - goods which have costs to society and consumption is harmful AND consumers are often unaware as to how harmful they are e.g. smoking.

Public goods - goods which display the characteristics of non-excludability and non-rivalry e.g. street lights. They will not be provided by the free market.

Private goods - they are excludable and have rivalry, most goods are private goods e.g. chocolate.

Quasi public good - goods which have the characteristics of a public good to a certain extent e.g. a park is non-excludable and non-rivalry but when it becomes very busy it becomes rivalrous.

Symmetric information/perfect information - buys and sellers both have all the information and the same information.

Asymmetric information/lack of perfect information - sometimes sellers have more information than buyers e.g. used car sales person. The seller knows the faults but does not tell the buyer.

Imperfect information - when buyers and/or sellers do not have all the information to make a decision e.g. consumers are not fully aware of the harm of smoking so they overconsume.
NB if there is asymmetric information there will be imperfect information.

Inequality *(AQA only)* - unequal distribution of income eg a doctor earns more than a nurse.

External Cost and Benefit

When there are negative externalities (external cost) eg noise, the social costs (cost to the individual and 3rd party) are higher than the private cost.

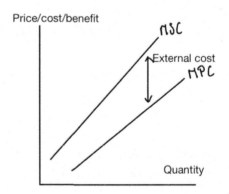

When there are positive externalities (external benefit) e.g. enjoying the flowers in another persons garden, the social benefit (benefit to the individual and benefit to 3rd party) will be higher than the private benefit.

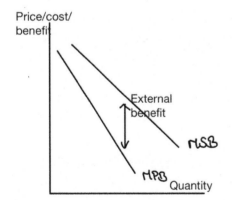

Externality Diagrams

Negative Production Externalities eg a chemical factory

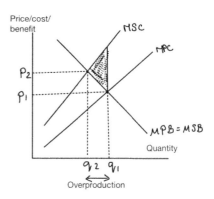

Price/cost/benefit

MSC

MPC

P2

P1

MPB = MSB

Quantity

q2 q1

Overproduction

If producer only considers the costs to themselves they will produce at p1q1. This is where they take into account private costs and benefits. If they were to consider the costs to the 3rd party e.g. pollution they would produce at p2q2.   They are overproducing by q2-q1. Due to this overproduction there is a welfare loss of the shaded triangle.

Positive Consumption Externalities e.g. education

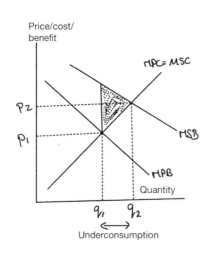

Price/cost/benefit

MPC= MSC

P2

MSB

P1

MPB

Quantity

q1   q2

Underconsumption

If the consumer only considers the benefits to themselves of education they will consume at p1q1. This is where they take into account private costs and benefits. If they were to consider the benefits to the 3rd party e.g. greater productivity, they would produce at p2q2.   They are underconsuming by q2-q1. There is a welfare gain (shaded triangle) which could be achieved if consumption is at the optimal level of q2.

The next two diagrams are for AQA and OCR only. These diagrams are a bit confusing. They key point to remember is that the cost curve is relevant to suppliers / production. The demand curve is relevant to consumers/ consumption.

Negative Consumption Externalities eg smoking

If consumers only consider the benefits to themselves they will consume at p1q1. This is where they take into account private costs and benefits. The benefits to society are lower than to the individual - there are dis benefits. If social benefits are considered they will consume at p2q2. They are overconsuming by q2-q1. Due to this overconsumption there is a welfare loss of the shaded triangle.

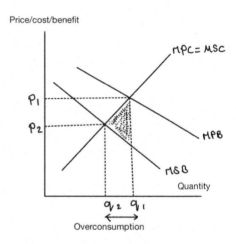

Positive Production Externalities e.g. the council building a bus shelter provides shelter from the rain so people don't need to go into a coffee shop and spend money thus lowering costs to the 3rd party.

If producers only consider the costs and benefits to themselves they will produce at p1q1. This is where they take into account private costs and benefits. The costs to society are lower than to the individual because the 3rd party is saving money due to the production of the bus shelter. If social costs are considered they will produce at p2q2. They are underproducing by q2-q1. The shaded triangle shows the welfare gain which they are missing out on by producing at q1.

Inequality *(AQA only for year 12, other exam boards do this in year 13)*

Why is there Inequality
1. Some people earn more than others - more skills allows a person to earn more.
2. Inheritance / lottery win.
3. Investments e.g. shares, property.

Government Intervention to Reduce Inequality
1. Progressive taxation e.g. income tax in the UK.
2. Proving free health care and education.
3. Benefits such as JSA and child benefit.
4. Free school lunches.

Chapter 7 Government Intervention - Taxes and Subsidies

Definitions

Indirect tax - tax on goods and services e.g. VAT.

Direct tax - tax on income e.g. income tax.

Specific/unit tax - fixed rate tax e.g. £1 per bottle of wine.

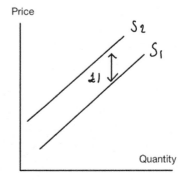

Ad valorem tax - a % tax e.g. 15% on a bottle of wine so more tax is paid for a more expensive bottle.

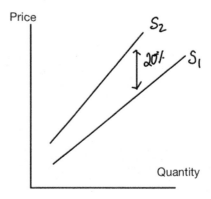

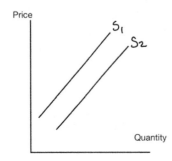

Subsidy - money paid to producers to encourage production, often for goods with positive externalities eg sports facilities.

Taxation

A tax is often used to reduce consumption of goods with negative externalities e.g. smoking.

- A tax increases the cost of production shifting the supply curve from S1 to S2.
- Price increases from P1 to P2.
- Quantity falls from Q1 to Q2 which corrects the market failure of overconsumption.
- The amount of tax paid by the consumer is the top rectangle.
- The amount of tax paid by the producer is the bottom rectangle.
- When demand is inelastic there is a small reduction in quantity so the tax is not as effective.
- When demand is inelastic a larger proportion of the tax is paid by the consumer.

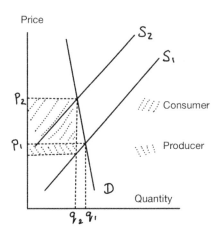
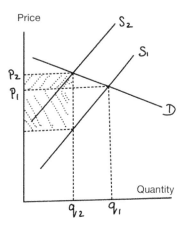

-

Advantages of Taxation

1. Consumption is reduced so the negative externality is reduced.
2. Those responsible for the negative externality are paying for it - the externality is internalised.
3. Government gets tax revenue which they can use to pay debt or spend on providing information to persuade smokers to reduce consumption, thus reducing the externality.

Disadvantages of Taxation
1. Ineffective if demand is inelastic.
2. Placing a monetary value on the externality is difficult so the market failure might not be fully corrected.
3. Cost of production is increased for firms so they become less internationally competitive which could lead to firms closing down and unemployment.
4. Firms may relocate abroad to avoid the tax.
5. The money received might not be used to correct the externality.

Subsidy
Used to encourage the consumption of merit goods eg swimming pools

- A subsidy decreases the cost of production shifting S1 to S2.
- Price falls from P1 to P2.
- Quantity increases from q1 to q2 which corrects the market failure of underconsumption.
- The gain from the subsidy by the producer is the top rectangle.
- The gain from the subsidy by the consumer is the bottom rectangle.
- When demand is inelastic there is a small increase in quantity so the subsidy is not as effective.
- When demand is inelastic a larger proportion of the subsidy goes to the producer.

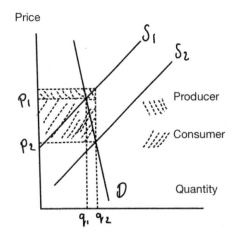
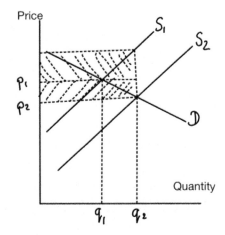

Advantages of Subsidies

1. Increased consumption of goods with positive externalities.
2. Price of the good falls.
3. Subsidies can help infant industries until they are established enough to survive.

Disadvantages of subsidies

1. There will be an opportunity cost - the money could have been spent on something else.
2. It is difficult to place a monetary value on the positive externalities so the market failure might not be fully corrected.
3. Producers may rely on subsidies and have no incentive to be more efficient.
4. If PED is inelastic the quantity will not increase by very much.

Chapter 8 Government Intervention - Price Controls

Definitions
Maximum price/price ceiling - the highest price a producer can sell a good, set below equilibrium to increase consumption e.g. rent controls.

Minimum price/price floor - suppliers must not sell below this price, set above equilibrium e.g. agricultural products to ensure producers get a fair price.

Maximum price

- Aims to increase consumption of merit or necessary goods by reducing the price.
- Can be used to prevent monopolies exploiting consumers.
- Can help those on low incomes afford essential goods.
- Will only be effective if the price is below equilibrium.

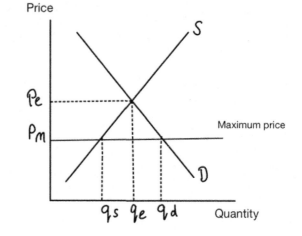

- Price is set at Pm.
- The amount suppliers are willing to supply falls to qs
- The amount consumers are willing to buy increases to qd
- There will be a shortage/excess demand of qd-qs.
- There will be a smaller excess if the PED and PES are inelastic (steeper curves).
- Some people who need the product may now not be able to get it due to the limited supply.
- A black market may develop - those who are able to get the product sell it on at a higher price.

Minimum Price

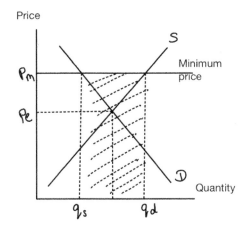

- Aims to ensure suppliers get a fair price by increasing the price.
- Will only be effective if above equilibrium.
- Ensures producers have a guaranteed minimum income if the government buys the surplus.
- Stockpiles of surplus can be sold in times of shortage.
- Price is set at Pm.

- The amount suppliers are willing to supply increases to qs.
- The amount consumers are willing to buy falls to qd.
- There will be a surplus of qd-qs.
- The shortage will be smaller if PED and PES are inelastic.
- If this is a guaranteed minimum price the government will buy the surplus at the guaranteed price.
- The cost to the government/taxpayer will be the shaded area.
- There will be an opportunity cost of this increased government spending.
- The surplus could be wasted if it cannot be stored for future years.
- Inefficient allocation of resources as more is produced than is required.

Buffer stocks _(OCR only)_

- Buffer stock schemes aim to stabilise prices.
- Used where supply is unpredictable so prices fluctuate.
- The aim is to ensure suppliers have a stable income.
- Will only work for commodes which can be stored e.g. wheat.
- A range of prices is set, the commodity is bought if there is too much supply and sold from the buffer stock if there is a shortage.

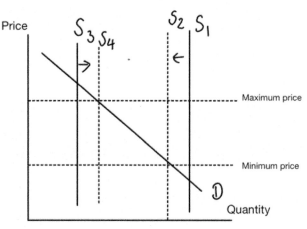

- If supply is S1 the price falls below the minimum threshold.
- The government steps in to buy up the shortage so that supply to the market is now S2 and the price rises to the minimum price.
- If there is low supply of S3 this would push the price above the maximum.
- The government would release some supply from the buffer stock so the supply is now S4 and the price falls to the maximum price.

Problems with Buffer Stocks

- The good harvests and bad harvests are not always the same size so when there is a shortage there might not be enough buffer stock to fill the gap.
- Storage is costly.
- Produces may overproduce due to the guaranteed price.
- If the minimum price is too high the government might spent a lot buying the excess supply.

Chapter 9 Privatisation, Regulation and Deregulation

Definitions
Privatisation - selling a state owned business to the private sector, often splitting it into parts e.g. British Rail.

Contracting out - the government pays a private firm to do part of a job eg catering or cleaning in schools.

Regulation - rules set by the government e.g. no smoking in public places.

Deregulation - removing rules e.g. removing rules about who can compete in markets.

Privatisation
The aim is to improve efficiency by selling the state owned firm and splitting it into parts. This is a key supply side policy used by Thatcher. Examples in the UK are British Rail, British Gas, British Telecom.

Advantages of Privatisation
1. Increased competition improves efficiency.
2. Lower prices.
3. Raises money for the government.
4. More choice for consumers.

Disadvantages of Privatisation
1. If the privatised firm remains a monopoly it may exploit consumers.
2. Less attention to safety.
3. Government has less/no control over how it is run so may not be in consumers interests.

Regulations
These are used in many situations often to correct market failure and to protect consumers. Examples of regulation are
- Compulsory face masks indoors.
- Banning smoking in public places.
- Age restrictions on buying alcohol.
- Compulsory child booster seats.

- Energy companies must use a certain percentage of renewable energy.
- Workers maximum working weak and minimum required breaks.

Advantages of Regulation
1. Encourages consumption of merit goods.
2. Discourages the use of demerit goods.
3. Encourages use of green energy.
4. Safer working conditions.
5. Protection of human rights.
6. Higher standards.

Disadvantages of Regulation
1. Often needs policing which costs.
2. Difficult to get the level correct / appropriate.
3. Can be expensive for firms to meet the regulations so prices may rise or they may go out of business.
4. Could encourage a black market e.g. people illegally selling cigarettes.

Deregulation
Deregulation removes or reduces rules making competition easier for firms. Examples could be allowing other firms to compete with Royal Mail or removing the rule of wearing face masks in public places. Deregulation may remove barriers to entry making it easier for new firms to join the market.

Advantages of Deregulation
1. The market becomes more contestable (more competition due to the low barriers to entry).
2. Improve efficiency as less hoops for firms to jump through (red tape).
3. Can reduce costs for firms.
4. Customers have more choice.

Disadvantages of Deregulation
1. Product quality may be lower due to fewer restrictions.
2. Increased negative externalities if pollution laws removed.
3. Safety may be compromised.
4. Less protection for consumers.

Chapter 10 Other Government Intervention and Government Failure

Definitions
State provision - government providing certain goods and services eg education.

Information provision - government providing information to influence consumption e.g. encouraging people to have the covid vaccine.

Tradeable pollution permits *(OCR only)* - permits to pollute up to a certain level. If they are not required they can be sold.

Government Failure - when the government intervenes to correct a market failure but makes a situation worse eg guaranteed minimum price to farmers will lead to large stockpiles which get wasted.

State Provision
- Governments use taxes to provide goods and services free of charge.
- These tend to be merit goods such as education and NHS or public goods which would otherwise not be provided eg street lights.
- The aim is to reduce the market failure of underconsumption.

Advantages of State Provision.
1. Reduces inequality as everyone has access to the goods.
2. Reduces market failure of underconsumption.
3. Redistributes income as tax is used to pay for the goods.
4. Healthier and better educated population.

Disadvantages of State Provision.
1. Higher taxes required to pay for state provision.
2. People who can afford to pay for themselves get the goods free of charge.
3. Less incentive for these goods to be provided efficiently as no profit motive for the government.
4. Deciding how much to provide is difficult eg too much then it is overconsumed/ wasted, too little there will be long waiting lists.

Information Provision
- Giving consumers more information enables them to make an informed and rational choice about consumption.
- Reduces the asymmetric information e.g. compulsory food labelling allows consumers to see the sugar and fat content of foods before buying, this may encourage them to make different / better choices.
- Information provision will impact the demand for a product. E.g. providing information on the benefits of fruit and vegetables will shift demand to the right for fruit and vegetables. Providing information on the damaging effect of too much sugar will shift the demand curve for sugary products like chocolate to the left.

Tradeable Permits
- The government puts a limit on the amount of pollution allowed and give permits to firms to pollute up to this level.
- Permits can be bought and sold, those who don't need them sell to those who need to pollute more.
- If firms exceed their allowance they will be fined.
- Each year the allowance is reduced so firms have to gradually cut their pollution and change production methods.

Advantages of Tradeable Permits
1. Firms are encouraged to reduce pollution as they can sell permits they don't need.
2. Governments get revenue from fines.
3. The scheme internalises the externality as those polluting more pay more (by buying unused permits).
4. If the level is set correctly pollution should be reduced overall.

Disadvantages of Tradeable Permits
1. Difficult to pick the appropriate optimal level of pollution. Too high will not be effective. Too low firms may be forced to close or relocate.
2. Expensive to police and administer.
3. Firms which were at or just below the limit have no incentive to reduce pollution even though they could do so cheaply.
4. The higher polluting firms may have very high costs associated with reducing pollution, it may be cheaper overall for the smaller firms to each reduce pollution be a lesser amount.

Government Failure *(not needed in year 12 for CIE)*

- Government failure can lead to a net welfare loss as intervention can create different problems.
- Rent controls (maximum rent) means that landlords may sell their properties so there will then be a shortage or housing available to rent.
- Increasing income tax to raise revenue acts as a disincentive to work/work extra hours.
- Subsidies remove the incentive for firms to improve efficiency as the government is giving them money for free.
- Government failure is often due to insufficient information eg bringing in laws could encourage a black market for that good if it is especially desirable.

Chapter 11 Cost, Revenue and Profit

AQA only for year 12, other exam boards do this in year 13

Definitions and Equations

Short run - the period of time in where least one factor of production is fixed.

Long run - all factors of production are variable.

Fixed costs - costs which do not increase when output increases eg rent.

Variable costs - costs which increase when output increases eg ingredients.

Total cost = fixed costs + variable costs.

Average cost = total cost / quantity.

Total Revenue/ Turnover = Price x Quantity

Average Revenue = Total Revenue / Price.

Profit = Total revenue - Total cost.

Economies of Scale - lower average costs for a firm when they increase their scale of production.

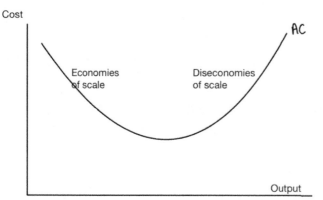

Diseconomies of scale - increased average costs when the first gets too big.

Internal Economies of Scale -cost advantages due to the firm growing in size
- Purchasing economies - larger firms can buy raw materials in bulk and negotiate discounts which will lower the cost per unit.

- Financial economies - larger firms will be less of a risk to banks so likely get a lower interest rate on loans.
- Risk-bearing economies - larger firms can diversify into different markets or different countries to spread risks. If one product is doing badly another would hopefully be doing well. E.g. supermarkets used to just sell food now they have phone shops, currency and pharmacies.
- Marketing economies - larger firms have a bigger marketing budget so can advertise at football matches for example. A larger firm can advertise several products as part of the brand at the same time. This means the per unit advertising cost is lower.
- Managerial economies - as the firm grows the number of managers does not grow so the manager cost per unit falls. Larger firms can afford to employ specialists who will be more qualified/ more efficient.
- Technical economies - larger firms can spend on specialist equipment which is faster and lowers unit cost. A bigger lorry which can deliver 4 times as much is not going to cost 4 times as much and will still only require one driver so the unit costs of delivery will fall.

External Economies of Scale - cost advantages due to the firm being part of a growing industry.
- Many firms in one location can share resources such as waste disposal.
- Suppliers of raw materials may locate nearby.
- Local training courses may locate nearby so there will be a large pool of skilled workers.
- There may be a better transport network making deliveries easier as well as easier for workers to get to work.
- Shared research and development facilities.

Diseconomies of Scale
- Communication problems - harder to communicate when there are more people, workers might not be clear about what they should be doing.
- Managers will have less control as the firm grows.
- More wastage as materials may get lost in a bigger warehouse.
- Co-ordination problems - might be harder to co-ordinate between departments.
- Lower motivation - workers may feel less valued so lower productivity.

Chapter 12 Competitive Markets

AQA only for year 12, other exam boards do this in year 13

Definitions

Differentiated product - products are slightly different eg Cadburys buttons are different to Asda buttons.

Homogeneous product - all products are exactly the same.

Barriers to entry - obstacles which make it hard for new firms to enter the market e.g. high set up costs.

Sunk costs - costs which cannot be recovered if a firm exits the market e.g. advertising or depreciation on a vehicle.

Concentration ratio - the % of the market which the largest firms take up. E.g. the 4 firm concentration ratio is the % the 4 largest firms take up.

Non-price competition - when firms are not focused on competing on price but offer other things e.g. loyalty card; after sales service; better quality product.

Perfect Competition
- A theoretic form of competition.
- No barriers to entry or exit.
- Homogenous product.
- Many buyers and sellers.
- Firms are price takers.
- Perfect knowledge.
- Lower prices than other forms of competition.

Monopolistic Competition.
- No or low barriers to entry or exit.
- Differentiated product.
- Many buyers and sellers.
- Firms have some price making power.
- E.g. restaurants and clothing stores.

Oligopoly
- High barriers to entry
- Differentiated product.
- A few large firms dominate the market.
- Firms are price makers
- E.g. mobile phones and supermarkets.

Monopoly
- High barriers to entry.
- Unique product (pure monopoly).
- Differentiated (monopoly power).
- One large firm dominates the market (pure monopoly).
- Firms are price makers.
- Firms tend to charge higher prices due to lack of competition.
- A legal monopoly has 25% or more market share.
- Large output so large economies of scale.

Alternative of Firms
Profit maximisation is a key objective of most firms. Sometimes firms will have other objectives:
- Revenue maximisation - this might be to help with cash flow
- Sales maximisation - when breaking into a new market; to increase market share; force a competitor out or sell off old stock.
- Survival - in a recession or if the firm is new.
- Charities - they have a variety of objectives depending on their cause eg water aid is to provide clean water.

Chapter 13 The Circular Flow of Income and the Multiplier

Definitions

Circular flow of income - flow of incomes, expenditure and output between firms and households.

Injections - money entering the circular flow of income - investment, government spending and exports.

Withdrawals - money leaving the circular flow of income - saving, taxation and imports.

Marginal propensity to consume (mpc) - proportion of additional income which is spent (change in consumption/change in income).

Marginal propensity to save (mps) - proportion of additional income which is saved (change in saving/change in income).

Marginal propensity of taxation (mpt) - proportion of additional income which is taxed (change in tax paid/change in income).

Marginal propensity to import (mpm) - proportion of additional income spent on imports (change in import spending/change in income).

Average propensity to consume (apc) - proportion of total income spent (total consumption/total income).

Average propensity to save (apc) - proportion of total income saved (total saving/total income).

The multiplier (k) - the amount an injection into the circular flow of income is multiplied by to find the final increase in national income (1/mpm+mps+mpt).

Wealth - value of all assets including income.eg property.

The Circular Flow of Income

Households provide land, labour and capital.

In return they receive money in the form of rent, wages and profit known as **national income**.

Firms produce goods and services, known as **national output**.

Households spend their money on these goods and services, known as **national expenditure**.

The above explains the circular flow of income.

National income = national output = national expenditure.

Injections into the circular flow will increase national income.

Withdrawals from the circular flow will decrease national income.

If injections are greater than withdrawals national income will increase.

The Multiplier

If the value of the multiplier is 5 this means that when there is an injection into the circular flow of income e.g. investment, the final increase in national income will be 5 times bigger than the investment.

A higher value for the multiplier will lead to a bigger final increase in national income.

The size of the multiplier is determined by the withdrawals from the circular flow of income.

$K = 1/ (mpm+mpt+mps)$

Changes in the Size of the Multiplier

- Increase in the exchange rate will make imports cheaper so more goods will be imported, mpm will increase which means more leakages so smaller value of the multiplier
- Increase in income tax will mean a greater proportion of income is taxed, mpt will increase so the multiplier will decrease.
- Increase in interest rates will encourage saving, mps will increase so the multiplier will decrease.

Chapter 14 Aggregate Demand, Aggregate Supply and Macroeconomic Equilibrium

Definitions

Aggregate demand - total spending on goods and services (AD = C + I + G + X - M)

Consumption - consumers spending on goods and services.

Investment - firms spending on capital goods e.g. vehicles and machinery.

Government spending - government spending on goods e.g. schools and hospitals.

Exports - money flowing into the country e.g. buying goods from abroad

Imports - money flowing out of the country e.g. to buy foreign goods.

Net Exports - exports – imports

Aggregate supply - total output of an economy.

Macroeconomic equilibrium - AS = AD.

Budget deficit - government spending it greater than tax revenue.

Budget surplus - government spending is less than tax revenue.

Balanced budget - government spending is equal to tax revenue.

The Aggregate Demand Curve

Note the axes are different to the micro axes.

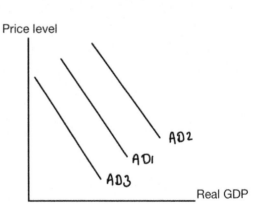

Factors Shifting the AD curve

If any of the components of AD change the AD curve will shift. e.g.
- **Increase in interest rates** AD1-AD3

More incentive to save, less incentive to consume.

Less investment and spending due to cost of borrowing increasing
- **Increase in income** AD1-AD2

More spending (C)
- **Increase in corporation tax** AD1-AD3

Less profit for firms to less investment.
- **Unemployment increases** AD1-AD3

People have less income so less spending, less profit for firms so less investment
- **Quality of UK goods improves** AD1-AD2

More demand for UK goods, less demand for foreign goods.
- **Consumer confidence increases** AD1-AD2

Consumers more prepared to spend, firms more prepared to invest.
- **Value of the pound increases** AD1-AD3

UK goods become more expensive; imports become cheaper.

Short Run Aggregate Supply Curve (SRAS)

Shifts in SRAS
If **COSTS** of production change
- **Increase in costs of production** e.g. wages, rent materials will shift SRAS to the left SRAS1 to SRAS2
- **Increase in oil price** will have a knock on effect on costs of production so shift SRAS to the left.
- **Decrease in the value of the pound** will make imported raw materials more expensive so increase cost of production shifting SRAS left.
- **Increased tax/reducing subsidies** will increase cost of reduction shifting SRAS to the left.

Long Run Aggregate Supply Curve (LRAS)

Monetarist LRAS
Monetarists believe that in the long run the economy will always tend towards full employment

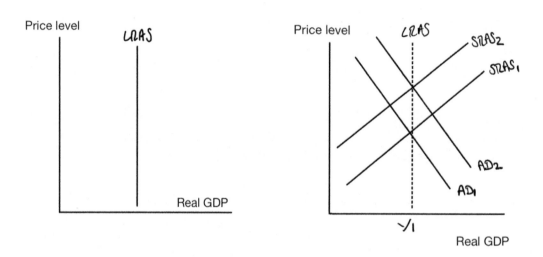

If AD increases e.g. due to reduction in interest rates AD1 shifts right to AD2. This leads to an increase in the price level. Workers now demand pay rises in order to maintain their real income. This will increase costs of production for firms so SRAS1 shifts to the left to SRAS2. There will be a further increase in the price level. Real output has returned to Y1.

Keynesian LRAS

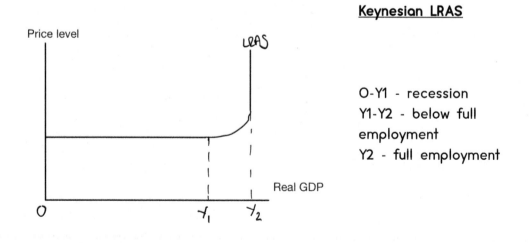

O-Y1 - recession
Y1-Y2 - below full employment
Y2 - full employment

Shifts in LRAS

If **FACTORS** of production change - an increase in the quantity or quality of resources will shift LRAS to the right from LRAS1 to LRAS2

- Improvements in technology
- More machinery/capital
- Training workers
- Relaxing rules on immigration
- Discovery of new resources

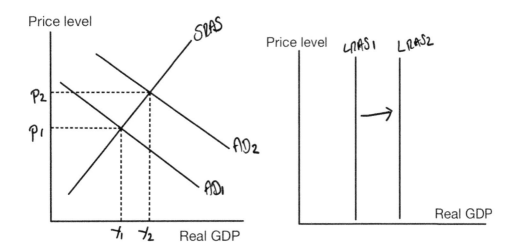

Macroeconomic Equilibrium

If there is an increase in AD eg due to a fall in interest rates AD1 shifts to the right to AD2.
Price level increases from P1 to P2.
This is demand-pull inflation.
Real GDP increases from Y1 to Y2.
This is economic growth.
More goods being produced means more workers needed because labour is a derived demand. Unemployment falls.
Due to higher price of UK goods exports will fall.
Due to more spending there will be more spent on imports. This will worsen the current account of the balance of payments.

If there is an increase in aggregate supply e.g. due to a fall in oil prices
SRAS1 shifts to SRAS2.
Price level falls from P1 to P2.
Real output increases from Y1 to Y2 which represents economic growth.
Increased output requires more workers. Unemployment falls.
UK goods become more competitive. The current account of the balance of payments improves.

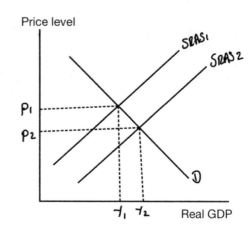

Using the Keynesian LRAS curve

The outcome of a policy will depend on the state of the economy.
Eg a reduction in income tax
In a recession AD1-AD2
Economic growth will increase
Unemployment will decrease
Inflation stays the same

Below full employment AD3-AD4
Economic growth increases
Unemployment decreases
Inflation increases

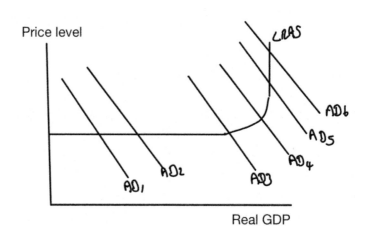

Full employment AD5-AD6
Economic growth no change
Unemployment no change
Inflation Increases

Eg Improvement in technology

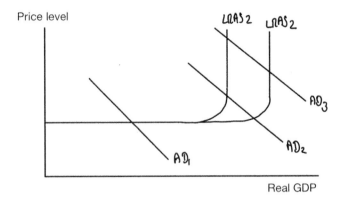

Price level · LRAS 2 · LRAS 2 · AD₃ · AD₂ · AD₁ · Real GDP

In a recession AD1

No change in any of the economic indicators

Below full employment AD2

Economic growth increases
Unemployment decreases
Inflation decreases

Full employment AD3

Economic growth increases
Unemployment decreases
Inflation decreases

Chapter 15 Economic Growth and Development

Definitions
Economic growth - increase in the productive potential of an economy.

GDP per capita - national income per person.

Real GDP - national income adjusted for inflation.

Recession - two successive quarters of negative economic growth.

Boom - when the economy is growing quickly.

Long run growth - an increase in the trend rate of growth.

Output gap - the difference between actual growth and potential growth.

Economic development -measuring the level of social and human welfare/quality of life.

GNI - GDP plus net income from abroad.

PPP - purchasing power parity; figures are adjusted to take into account cost of living in different countries.

Problems with Comparing Living Standards between Countries and over Time
1. The size of the hidden economy may differ eg car washing for a parent, babysitting for a friend, illegal trading.
2. Does not account for income inequality
3. Does not take into account hours worked
4. Quality of life not considered e.g. long commute to work or greater pollution levels.
5. Spending by the government varies e.g. in some countries education is free.
6. Different methods of calculation.

The Economic Cycle

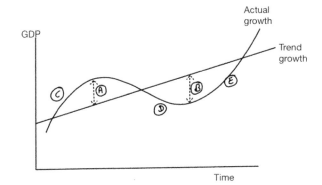

A - positive output gap
B - negative output gap
C - boom
D - recession
E - recovery

Benefits of Economic Growth
1. Wages are usually rising so higher standards of living.
2. Higher wages so increased spending, more profit for firms.
3. Higher wages, more income tax for government.
4. More profit for firms leads to more investment.
5. More profit for firms means more tax revenue.
6. More demand for goods leads to more demand for labour so reduced unemployment.
7. Firms have more money so may invest in greener technology.
8. Greater tax revenue for the government and less need to spend on benefits so there may be a budget surplus which can be used to pay back national debt.

Costs of Economic Growth
1. Inequality may increase as often the rich are getting richer.
2. Finite resources get used up so may increase in price.
3. Habitats are destroyed.
4. Negative externalities due to increased production.
5. Working hours may be longer.
6. If supply cannot keep up with demand there will be demand pull inflation.
7. Increased income means increased spending on imports worsening the balance of payments.

Short run and Long Run Economic Growth

Short run growth is achieved if there is an increase in AD eg lower interest rates or an increase in SRAS e.g. lower costs of production.

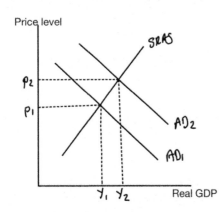 

Long run growth is achieved through increasing the quantity and quality of resources eg investing in new technology or increased education and training.

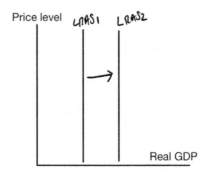

Economic Growth and the PPC

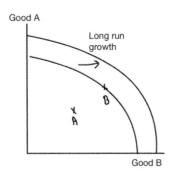

Short run growth - A to B
Long run growth - shift of the PPC

Measures of Development

GNI per capita PPP
This is GDP including income from abroad per person, adjusted for cost of living in different countries.

Human Development Index (HDI)
This has three elements. Each is given a score; these are combined to give an overall value between 0 and 1 with 1 being the most developed
- Income - GNI per capita PPP
- Education -means and expected years of schooling
- Heath - life expectancy at birth

Problems with HDI
1. More years of schooling doesn't mean good quality education.
2. Attendance at school might be poor.
3. Long life expectancy does not mean good quality of life.
4. GNI per capita does not take into account the hidden economy.
5. Inequity is not taken into account.

Other Measures of Development
1. % of workforce in agriculture.
2. Number of mobile phones per 1000 of the population.
3. % of households with access to clean water.
4. Gender inequality.

Chapter 16 Employment and Unemployment

Definitions

The level of unemployment - number of people looking for a job who do not have a job.

The rate of unemployment - the number unemployed as a % of the labour force.

Claimant count - number of people claiming unemployment related benefits.

The Labour force survey (ILO) - uses a sample of the population to count those who are out of work and actively seeking work.

Full employment - where everyone of working age who wants to work has a job at the current wage rate.

Underemployment - when someone has a job but the job does not fully utilise their skills or when someone is working part time but wants to work full time.

Frictional unemployment - unemployment for a short period of time between jobs.

Seasonal unemployment - unemployment due to the season eg ski instructors will be unemployed in the summer.

Cyclical unemployment - unemployment due to the economy being in the recession stage of the economic cycle.

Structural unemployment - unemployment due to the change in structure of the economy e.g. coal mines closing down.

Measures of Unemployment

The two methods will give slightly different numbers because some people will be in one count but not the other.

Claimant count - includes those who are illegally claiming benefits.

ILO survey - includes those who are unemployed but not able to claim benefits due to savings being too high or partner working.

Problems of Unemployment
1. Lower incomes, less spending power, lower standard of living
2. Fewer goods and services produced, less profit for firms.
3. Firms have less money for investment.
4. The government will need to spend more on benefits.
5. Increased levels of crime, depression and family break ups.
6. Less tax revenue for the government from income tax, VAT and corporation tax.

Policies to Reduce Unemployment
1. Reduce interest rates to increases AD.
2. Reduce taxation eg income tax so people have more money to spend.
3. Education and training to improve occupational immobility.
4. Subsidies to firms to encourage them to invest in areas of high unemployment.
5. Lower minimum wage so firms can afford to employ more workers.

Chapter 17 Inflation

Definitions
Inflation - a sustained rise in the average price level/fall in the value of money.

Deflation - a fall in average price level.

Disinflation - the rate or inflation is falling but prices are still rising.

Hyperinflation - very high inflation.

Measures of Inflation
Consumer Price Index (CPI)
This is the main measure used in the UK. The target rate of inflation in the UK is 2%. The price of a typical basket of goods is calculated. In the base year this is given the value 100. Inflation for the year is calculated by recalculating the price of the basket of goods. Items in the basket of goods is updated regularly to reflect trends e.g. hand gel was added recently.

Retail Price Index (RPI)
This tends to be higher than CPI as it includes mortgage interest payments and council tax.

Problems with CPI and RPI
1. Only a sample of the population is used.
2. Households may not record accurate information.
3. The basket of goods is only updated once a year eg hand gel was added in 2021 when there had been a significant increase in demand during 2020.

Types of Inflation

Demand-pull inflation

Caused when supply cannot keep up with
demand.   AD shifts to the right from AD1-AD2.
Price level increases from P1-P2

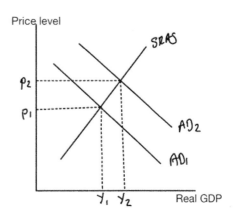

Examples:
- increased income
- reduced income tax
- reduction in interest rates
- high consumer confidence
- increased demand for exports
-

Cost-push inflation

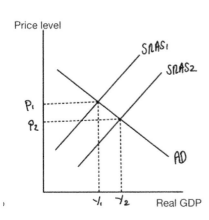

Caused due to increased costs of production.
SRAS1 shifts to the right to SRAS2.

Examples:
- increased wages
- increased raw material prices
- imported raw material increase in price
- increased oil prices
- increased tax

Problems of Inflation

1. Cost of living increases so consumers can buy fewer goods and services.
2. Workers may ask for pay rises so cost of production increases leading to further inflation.
3. Shoe leather costs - cost of searching for the best prices in a climate of rising prices.

4. Menu costs - costs of updating prices lists.
5. International competitiveness falls so fewer exports will be bought.
6. Uncertainty may mean less consumption and less investment.

Deflation

Although rising prices are generally not good, falling prices are undesirable in some situations.

1. If deflation is due to falling costs of production perhaps due to better technology this will not be a problem.
2. If deflation is due to low aggregate demand, firms may have to reduce prices to get rid of stock. This is undesirable.
3. Deflation generally means the economy is doing badly.
4. Lower prices means less profit for firms or possibly even loss if they are having to heavily discount old stock.

Usefulness of Inflation Figures

1. Employers use the figures to determine pay rises - pay needs to keep up with inflation otherwise workers will see a fall in their real wage.
2. Trade unions use the figures when bargaining for higher wages for their workers.
3. Government uses the figures to establish how much to increase pensions and benefits.

Chapter 18 The Balance of Payments

Definitions
Balance of payments - a record of a countries transactions with the rest of the world.

Current account - the difference between the value of exports of goods and services and the value of imports of goods and services.

Exports - money flowing into the country.

Imports - money flowing out of the country.

Current account surplus - exports are greater than imports.

Current account deficit - exports are less than imports.

Balance of payments disequilibrium - when there is a deficit or surplus.

Current Account
There are 4 sections:
1. Trade in goods e.g. clothes, cars
2. Trade in services e.g. employing a tutor based in another country, tourism.
3. Primary income - income from employment or investments e.g. dividends on shares in another country, profits from a company based abroad.
4. Secondary income - money moving between countries for which no work is done eg remittances (money sent home to family members when someone works abroad), foreign aid.

The UK usually has a large deficit on the current account.

Causes of a Deficit on the Current Account
1. UK goods are more expensive than goods abroad e.g. due to higher labour costs.
2. The quality of UK goods is worse than goods abroad.
3. Inflation is higher in the UK than other countries.

4. An increase in the exchange rate causes UK goods to be more expensive abroad.

Problems with a Current Account Deficit
1. There will be lower demand for UK goods which could lead to lower growth and loss of jobs.
2. Less demand for UK goods means less demand for pounds. This will lead to a fall in the exchange rate. Imported raw materials become more expensive. This could lead to cost push inflation.
3. The deficit needs to be funded by borrowing on the capital account. The borrowed money needs to be paid back with interest.
4. A deficit may suggest a country is uncompetitive.

When is a Deficit not a Problem
1. If it is small in comparison to national income.
2. If it is for a short period of time.

Policies to Correct Imbalances on the Current Account
These can be split into two categories
1. **Expenditure switching policies** - aim to switch spending from foreign goods to home produced goods.
- Restrictions on imports e.g. tariffs and quotas
- Subsidies to home firms to help them lower costs of production.
- Depreciate the exchange rate to make home produced goods cheaper abroad.
- Supply-side policies to encourage efficiency and reduce costs of production.

2. **Expenditure reducing policies** - aimed at reducing spending which will reduce spending on home produced goods as well as imports.
- Tight fiscal policy e.g. increasing income tax so consumers have less disposable income.
- Tight monetary policy e.g. increasing interest rates so consumers are less likely to spend.

Chapter 19 Fiscal Policy

Definitions

Fiscal policy - using government spending and taxation to influence aggregate demand.

Tight/deflationary fiscal policy - reducing government spending and increasing taxation to reduce aggregate demand.

Expansionary/reflationary fiscal policy - increasing government spending and reducing taxation to increase aggregate demand.

Discretionary fiscal policy - deliberate changes in taxation and government spending e.g. an increase in the rate of VAT.

Automatic stabilisers - changes in taxation and government spending which change automatically e.g. in a boom there will be more income tax, corporation tax and VAT. In a recession tax revenue will be lower due to fewer people working.

Capital government spending - spending on assets such as building schools or hospitals

Current government spending - day to day running of the assets eg teachers pay or medications.

Progressive tax - as income increases the % of income on this tax increases e.g. income tax in the UK.

Regressive tax - as income increases the % of income on this tax decreases e.g. car tax

Proportional tax - as income increases the % of income on this tax stays the same. e.g. VAT if everyone were to spend all of their income (unlikely).

Direct tax- tax on income e.g. income tax and corporation tax.

Indirect tax - tax on spending e.g. VAT and excise duty.

Marginal tax rate - tax rate on the last pound.

Budget deficit - government spending is greater than taxation in a year.

Budget surplus - government spending is less than taxation in a year.

Balanced budget - government spending and taxation are equal in a year.

National debt - accumulated budget deficits.

Cyclical budget deficit - over the economic cycle the budget deficit is cancelled out but the budget surplus.

Structural budget deficit - over the economic cycle the deficit is greater than the surplus.

Crowding out - an increase in government spending e.g. on schools means that there will be less demand for private schools so less investment in the private sector. The increase in government spending has led to a reduction in investment.

The Impact of Fiscal Policy on the Macro Economic Objectives

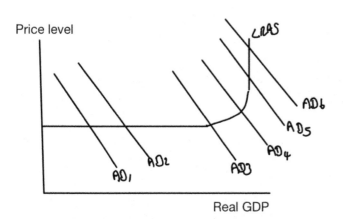

Expansionary fiscal policy is often used in a recession.

Increased G will increase AD because G is a component of AD.

Reduced income tax will increase C because consumers now have more money.

Reduced corporation tax will mean firms have more profit for Investment.

AD shifts to the right.

The impact on the economy depends on the state of the economy.

In a **recession** AD1 shifts to AD2. There will be in increase in output, this leads to an increase in employment due to derived demand for labour. Price level stays the same.

If the economy is **below full employment** AD3 shifts to AD4. There will be an increase in output and employment but an increase in price level. This means there is a trade-off. If inflation is low then a small increase will not be a problem.

At **full employment** AD5 shifts to AD6. There will be no change in output or employment but there will be an increase in the price level. This means that expansionary fiscal policy should not be used at full employment. Instead tight fiscal policy (AD6 - AD5) might be used to reduce AD and reduce the price level without having a knock on effect on employment or economic growth.

Budget Deficit
A budget deficit is also known as public sector net cash requirement (PSNCR) or public sector net borrowing (PSNB). They borrow this money from UK banks or by selling treasury bills. The money needs to be paid back with interest.

Problems with a Large Deficit
1. It needs to be paid back with interest which will be compounded.
2. If there is high government spending this could lead to inflation.
3. Higher inflation could lead to higher interest rates.
4. National debt will increase if the deficit is long term.
5. A large debt means that a country is less attractive to FDI.

Correcting a Deficit
1. Austerity measures e.g. reducing government spending or increase taxation - this will lead to a reduction in AD which could lead to recession.
2. Rely on automatic stabilisers - as the economy recovers more tax will be paid and there will be less need for the government to spend.

The Laffer Curve

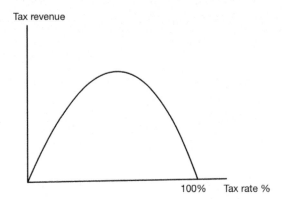

This shows that as the tax rate increases
initially more tax revenue will be collected.
Once tax gets to a certain level tax revenue
will decline because people will work fewer
hours or evade tax. When the tax rate is 100%
no one will work so no tax will be collected.

Chapter 20 Monetary Policy

Definitions
Monetary policy - manipulation of interest rates, the money supply and exchange rates to influence aggregate demand.

Tight/deflationary monetary policy - increasing interest rates to reduce aggregate demand.

Expansionary monetary policy - reducing interest rates to increase aggregate demand.

Interest Rates
In the UK interest rates are set by the Monetary Policy Committee (MPC) of the Bank of England. They meet once a month to discuss whether interest rates should be changed. They have been given a target of 2% inflation. As well as looking at what is happening to prices they also consider the following as these can impact on inflation:
- **House prices** - if house prices are increasing this could lead to increased consumer confidence so increase AD.
- **The value of the pound** - if the value of the pound is low this could lead to increased price of imported raw materials so imported inflation.
- **Output gaps** - if there is a positive output gap the economy may be over heating which could be inflationary.
- **Wages** - if wages are increasing consumption and therefore AD will increase.

How Interest Rates Impact Aggregate Demand
An increase in interest rates will:
- increase incentive to save due to higher returns which means less consumption.
- make it more expensive to take out loans e.g. for a new car or house extension so less consumption.
- increase interest payments on existing loans or mortgages (unless they are fixed rate) so less money to spend on other consumption.
- more expensive for firms to take out loans so less investment.
- lower consumer and business confidence so less consumption and investment.

- higher demand for saving money in UK banks by foreign citizens so increased demand for pounds. This will increase the exchange rate. Exports become more expensive so fall in exports. Imports become cheaper so rise in Imports.

All of the above lead to a reduction in AD. This is known as tight monetary policy.

Impact on the Macroeconomic Objectives
Just as with fiscal policy the impact depends on the state of the economy.

In a recession AD1-AD2
This would have an overall negative effect on the economy. Economic growth falls so less workers needed leading to an increase in unemployment. The price level stays the same.

Below full employment AD3-AD4
There will be a reduction in price level but economic growth falls and unemployment increases.

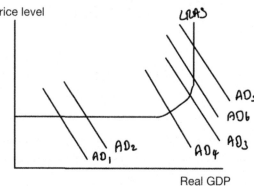

Full employment AD5-AD6
There will be a reduction in price level. Economic growth and unemployment stay the same so overall this is a positive outcome.

Problems with Monetary Policy
1. There is a time lag of approximately 2 years before the full effect is experienced.
2. Some indicators might suggest interest rates should increase eg house prices are increasing, others might suggest interest rates should decrease e.g. the economy is in a recession.
3. There will always be a trade off e.g. if interest rates are increased to increase economic growth this will be inflationary.
4. It is difficult to get accurate data on how much interest rates need changing by.

Quantitative Easing (QE)

This is a method of increasing the supply of money. Sometimes known as 'printing money' even though new money is not printed.

The central bank (Bank of England in the UK) buys assets eg bonds from commercial banks e.g. TSB. This means that commercial banks now have more money available to lend. If they lend more to customers then there will be more consumption so AD will increase.

Problems with QE

There might be more money available to lend but
1. Consumer confidence may be low so they might not want to borrow.
2. Those who do want to borrow might be high risk customers who the bank is unwilling to lend to.

Edexcel only
The Great Depression

This was a period of falling output, deflation and high unemployment around the world starting in the US in 1929 and lasting almost 10 years. Due to high unemployment there was less tax revenue but more spending on benefits so the budget deficit was large.

The decrease the deficit there were cuts in government spending which reduced AD making the recession worse.

In 1931 the UK left the gold standard so was now able to decrease interest rates which led to an increase in consumption and investment and therefore AD.

In the US taxes were low, they needed increasing due to low government revenue. In 1933 the new president increased government spending.

Financial Crisis 2008

A more Keynesian approach was used.
- Short term cut in VAT from 17.5% to 15% to increase consumption.
- Increased spending through automatic stabilisers.
- Bringing forward planning capital government spending.
- Expansionary monetary policy - interest rates were reduced to 0.5%.
- QE was used

The policies were effective but led to a large budget deficit and national debt. This was partly dealt with after the recession by large spending cuts and tax increases.

Chapter 21 Supply-side Policies

Definitions

Supply-side policies - policies aimed at increasing the productive potential of an economy.

Free market supply-side policies - polices to increase efficiency by removing things which prevent the free market from working e.g. privatisation, deregulation, improving labour market flexibility.

Interventionist supply-side policies - policies which aim to correct market failure e.g. spending on education, improving infrastructure.

Supply-side Policy Diagrams

Supply side policies will always aim to shift LRAS to the right. There would never be any circumstances in which the goal would be to shift LRAS to the left. Shifting LRAS to the left means that the maximum potential output has fallen.

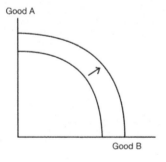

When supply side policies are implemented the PPC/PPF shifts outwards and LRAS shifts to the right.

Examples of Supply-side Policies

1. **Reduce unemployment benefits** - this will encourage more people to take a job, more people working increases the potential output.
2. **Reduce income tax** - this increases incentives for people who were not working to work as they now take home more of their earnings.

3. **Improve labour market flexibility** - making it easier for firms to make workers redundant when they are not needed means firms will be more willing to take on workers short term.
4. **Reduce power of trade unions** - less time lost through strikes.
5. **Improve education and training** - workers have more skills and will be more productive.
6. **Incentives for firms to invest** e.g. tax breaks - more investment e.g. in technology will increase productive capacity.
7. **Trade liberalisation** - removing barriers to trade between countries means goods and capital can be traded more freely.
8. **Privatisation** - selling state owned assets and splitting them into parts increases competition encouraging firms to be more productive.
9. **Deregulation** - removing rules can increase competition and improve efficiency.

Impact on the Macroeconomic Indicators

In a recession AD1
There will be no change to the equilibrium position so supply side policies are not very useful on their own.

Below full employment AD2
Economic growth increases
Employment increases
Inflation falls

Full employment AD3
Economic growth increases
Employment increases
Inflation falls

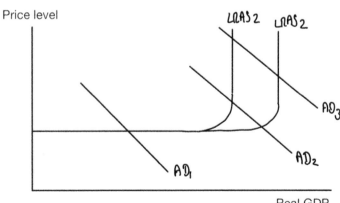

The current account of the balance of payments is likely to improve because lower prices will increase international competitiveness.

Supply-side Policies and AD

Some-side policies also shift AD:

- Encouraging firms to invest - investment is a component of AD so AD will shift right.
- Education and training will give people more skills so they can earn more money. They then spend more so consumption increases shifting AD to the right.

Problems with Supply-side Policies

1. There is usually a long time lag for them to fully take effect e.g. education can take many years.
2. Some policies are politically unacceptable e.g. reducing unemployment benefit.
3. Labour market reforms means workers have less job security.
4. Some policies lead to increased inequality e.g. cutting benefits.
5. They may be costly to implement so will have an opportunity cost to the government.

Chapter 22 Conflicts between Objectives

Definitions
Macroeconomic objectives - the four main goals are economic growth; reducing unemployment; low inflation (2%); equilibrium in balance of payments.

Trade-off - when making one indicator better another is made worse.

Conflicts when Shifting AD
E.g. interest rates are reduced to increase AD in order to achieve economic growth. The trade-off will be that prices rise. UK goods become less competitive so the current account of the balance of payments will worsen. More income means consumers spend more on imports which will also contribute to an worsening in the current account.

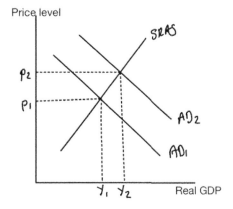

E.g. interest rates are increased to reduce AD and reduce inflation. The trade-off will be a reduction in economic growth and increase in unemployment. The current account of the balance of payments will improve because UK goods are more competitive and there is less spending so less spent on imports.

Economic Growth and the Environment
- More production means more pollution.
- New factories may be built on green land.
- More waste which needs disposing of due to increased production.
- Non renewable resources will be used up.
- Firms might spend increased profits on investment in green technology.

Economic Growth and Inequality
- Inequality will tend to increase i.e. the rich benefit most from the economic growth.

- When an economy grows high skilled workers are more in demand so wages will increase.
- Low skilled jobs may be replaced by machines so they become unemployed.
- Progressive taxation could be used to mitigate some of these effects.

Chapter 23 Exchange Rates and Terms of Trade

CIE only for AS level, other exam boards usually cover this at A level.

Definitions

(Nominal) Exchange rate - the value of one currency in terms of another.

Real exchange rate - nominal exchange rate adjusted to take into account cost of living in different countries.

Trade weighted exchange rate - exchange rate between a basket of other currencies weighted according to the amount of trade done with each country.

Fixed exchange rate - the value of one currency is fixed against another, the central bank needs to intervene to keep the rate at the agreed level.

Floating exchange rate - the rate changes when demand and supply of the currency change.

Depreciation - fall in value of a floating exchange rate.

Devaluation - fall in fixed value of the exchange rate.

Appreciation - rise in the value of a floating exchange rate.

Revaluation - rise in fixed value of the exchange rate.

Terms of trade - relative price of exports compared to imports.

Changes in the Value of a Floating Exchange Rate

Anything which causes the supply or demand for a currency to change will have an impact on the exchange rate. There will be an increase in the demand for pounds from D1 to D2 which increases the exchange rate.

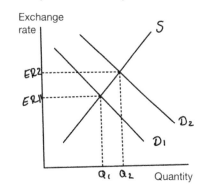

1. Incomes abroad increase so more demand for UK goods. Pounds are needed to buy UK goods.
2. Quality of UK goods improves so more demand for UK goods.
3. Interest rates in the UK increase. The flow of hot money into the UK to put into UK banks will increase.
4. Inflation in the UK is lower than other countries so increased demand for UK goods.
5. A major sporting event in the UK will increase the number of tourists who will need pounds.
6. Expectation that the value of the pound will increase. Speculators will buy pounds in order to sell when the value increases further.
7. Government increases the demand for pounds (they sell foreign reserves).

If there is an increase in supply of pounds there will be a decrease in the exchange rate.

1. UK incomes increase so more demand for imports. Pounds are supplied in exchange for foreign currency which is needed to buy the imports.
2. Quality of foreign goods improves so more demand for foreign goods. Supply of pounds increases in exchange for the foreign currency.

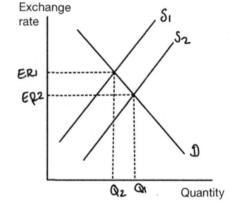

3. Interest rates in the UK fall. Hot money will leave the UK in search of higher interest rates, elsewhere.
4. Inflation in the UK is higher than other countries so there will be more demand for imports. Foreign currency is needed to buy the imports.
5. A major sporting event abroad so pounds are exchanged in exchange for foreign currency.
6. Speculators expect the value of the pound will fall so want to sell before it falls too low.
7. Government supplies pounds from their reserves and demands foreign currency.

Advantages of Floating Exchange Rate

1. No government intervention is needed to keep the exchange rate at a set level so less need for foreign reserves to manipulate the exchange rate.
2. Automatic correction of the balance of payments - if there is a deficit there will be less demand for pounds. This will reduce the exchange rate which makes UK goods cheaper so increases the demand for exports.
3. Monetary policy does not need to be used to keep the exchange rate at the agreed level. This means that monetary policy can be used to manage AD.

Disadvantages of Floating Exchange Rates

1. Planning is difficult for firms which import raw materials as the amount they have to pay is constantly fluctuating.
2. There may be less investment due to uncertainty over costs.
3. Speculators may 'bet' on what they expect to happen to the exchange rate which can cause large fluctuations.

Advantages of Fixed Exchange Rate

1. More certainty over costs of imported raw materials and trade with other countries so more investment and more trade.
2. Firms cannot rely on the exchange rate depreciating to make their goods cheaper abroad so they are forced to be more efficient.

Disadvantages of Fixed Exchange Rate

1. Monetary policy has to be used to keep the exchange rate at the fixed level so other tools need to be used to manage AD.
2. Government needs to keep large reserves of foreign currency in case they need to increase the value of the pound.
3. If the fixed rate is significantly over or under valued significant amounts of government intervention is needed to keep the current at the fixed rate.

Impacts on the Economy

A fall in the value of the pound will have the following impact:

- Exports become cheaper so demand will increase.
- Imports become more expensive so demand will fall.

- Net exports will increase.
- The current account of the balance of payments will improve.
- More demand for UK goods will shift AD right.
- Economic growth will increase.
- Labour is a derived demand so unemployment will fall.
- Inflation may increase.

The J curve and Marshall Lerner Condition
The above argument suggests that a fall in the value of the pound will lead to an improvement of the current account. However, this might not be the case.

If there is a fall in the value of the pound imported raw materials will become more expensive. Firms will still need to import the raw materials as they are essential for production. They will initially continue to buy the same quantity of materials but this quantity will cost them more. In the 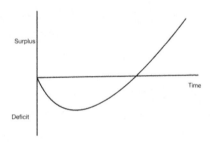 short term this means the current account will worsen as more is being spent on imports. In the longer term firms can find cheaper suppliers of raw materials or find suppliers in the home country. As they gradually replace these more expensive raw materials with cheaper alternatives the current account will improve. This is illustrated by the J curve.

The Marshall Lerner condition states that when there is a depreciation in the value of the currency there will be an improvement in the balance of payments if the PED for exports + PED for imports is greater than 1.

Terms of Trade
Terms of trade = (index of export prices / index of import prices) x 100

Terms of trade increases if export prices increase faster than import prices. This is known as an improvement in the terms of trade because the country can now buy more foreign goods with the money it gets from exports.

Chapter 24 Trade and Protectionism

CIE only for AS level, other exam boards usually cover this at A level.

Definitions

Absolute advantage - when a country is able to produce more of a product per unit of input than other countries.

Comparative advantage - when a country has a lower opportunity cost of producing a good than other countries.

Specialisation - countries focus on producing the goods they are best at.

Free trade area - no barriers to trade between countries within the area. Countries within the area impose their own barriers on other countries .

Customs union - free trade area but where all member countries impose the same barriers on other countries.

Monetary union - member have the same currency and common monetary policy eg Euro countries.

Protectionism - imposing barriers on countries to restrict imports and encourage purchase of local goods.

Tariff - tax on imported goods.

Quota - limit on the number of goods which can be imported.

Trade creation - when barriers are removed between two countries e.g. removing traffic there will be more trade due to the goods now being cheaper.

Trade diversion - when trade is diverted away from a country which is part of the union. The country has tariffs imposed making them more expensive.

Absolute and Comparative Advantage

Assumptions

- Only 2 countries
- All resources are fully and efficiently employed
- Resources can easily be switched from producing one good to producing the other (factor mobility).
- No transport costs.

	Tea		Coffee
Country A	120.	Or	80
County B	100.	Or	70

Country A has the absolute advantage in the production of both goods because it has a higher output of tea and of coffee.

To work out comparative advantage it is necessary to calculate opportunity cost ratios. This means working out what 1 unit of tea is worth for each country in terms of coffee.

Country A
To produce 120 units of tea they need to give up 80 units of coffee.
To produce 1 unit of tea they need to give up 80/120 units of coffee ie 0.67.

Country B
To produce 100 units of tea they need to give up 70 units of coffee.
To produce 1 unit of tea they need to give up 70/100 units of coffee ie 0.7.

Country A has the lowest opportunity cost so country A should produce tea because they need to give up less coffee. Country A has a comparative advantage in tea.
By default country B will produce coffee, country B will have the comparative advantage in coffee.
Note that a country is not able to have a comparative advantage in both goods.

Exchange Rate

Country A and B will need to trade with each other so they can both consume tea and coffee. The rate of exchange should be between (it does not need to be exactly half way) the two opportunity cost ratios in order for both countries to benefit. In this case an exchange rate of 1 tea = 0.68 coffee would mean both countries are better off if they specialise.

Advantages of Specialisation and Trade

1. Countries enjoy goods they are unable to produce due to the climate e.g. bananas and coffee cannot be produced in the UK.
2. Larger variety of goods can be enjoyed not just the ones produced at home.
3. Focusing on a small range of goods means countries can benefit from economies of scale to a greater extent.
4. Countries focus on the goods and services which they are best at.
5. Industries are able to grow and become more efficient.

Disadvantages of Specialisation and Trade

1. High transport costs.
2. Domestic industries will have more competition and may be forced out the market if they can't compete.
3. If there are political conflicts trade is disrupted.
4. If a country relies on another country for goods external factors such as Brexit, lack of lofty drivers, covid can make it difficult to get sufficient supply.

Trade Creation

Country A is the domestic country. The world equilibrium price of the good is P1 which is below the equilibrium price in country A. Country B trades with country A but there is a tariff on their goods. The tariff means that the price will be Pt. At this price domestic demand is Q3, domestic suppliers are prepared to supply Q2. The difference (Q3-Q2) is made up by importing from country B. Country A and B now join

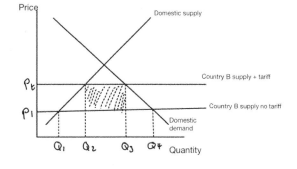

a customs union so the tariff is removed. This means that the price of goods from country B falls to P1. There will now be increased demand for the good (Q4). Domestic suppliers do not want to supply as much (Q1). The quantity imported will now be (Q4-Q1). Country A is now importing more tea from country B i.e. trade has been created. There will be a loss in tax revenue of the shaded area.

Trade Diversion

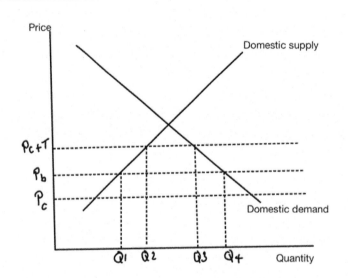

Country A is initially not part of a union. Country C is the most efficient producer. The price they charge is Pc but as a tariff is on the good the price the consumers in country A pay will be Pc+T. Domestic suppliers will supply Q2 but demand is Q3 so Q3-Q2 is imported from country C. Country A now forms a customs union with country B. This means that tariffs are now removed from country B meaning the price of goods from country B is now Pb. This makes country Bs goods cheaper than the more efficient country C so consumers will buy from country C. The demand will increases to Q4 due to the lower price. Domestic suppliers will supply Q1; Q4-Q1 will be imported. Trade has been diverted away from county C because it is not part of the union so has higher prices.

Reasons for Protectionism
1. Protect jobs in the home country - if foreign firms are cheaper, local firms might go out of business.
2. Ban certain goods eg the French banned British beef.
3. Ban trade from certain countries due to political disputes.
4. Protect infant industries in the home country whilst they are establishing themselves.

5. To avoid dependence on other countries - this can be a problem if there are disputes.
6. To prevent dumping - where countries their surplus supply of goods in another country to get rid of it at a price below cost of production. This may be done to try to force local firms out of the market.
7. To improve the current account of the balance of payments.
8. To raise tax revenue for the government.

Tariffs

In this market the domestic supply curve shows domestic suppliers willingness to supply at different prices. The world equilibrium price (P1) is lower than the equilibrium price in the home country. There will be an unlimited amount supplied at this price by other countries. The world supply curve will therefore be horizontal. As this price is significantly below the equilibrium price

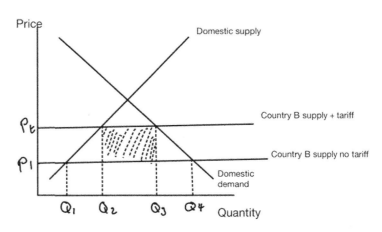

there will only be a small amount of local suppliers willing to supply (Q1). However, due to the low price the domestic demand will be high (Q4). This means that Q4-Q1 will need to be imported to make up the shortfall.

If a tariff is imposed this will increase the price of the imported goods to Pt. As the price has increased the domestic supply will increase to Q2. The higher price means that domestic demand will fall slightly to Q3. The shortfall is made up with imports. Imports will now be Q3-Q2.
Total tax revenue collected by the government is the shaded area (tax per unit x number of units imported).

Quotas

Quotas are a limit on the amount that a country will import from another country. The aim is to encourage consumers to purchase more home produced goods as there are fewer foreign goods available. As in the previous diagram the world supply is unlimited at a price of P1. Q1 is

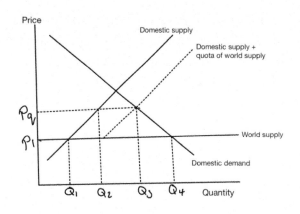

supplied by domestic suppliers, demand is Q4 so Q4-Q1 will be imported. A quota is now applied which is a set number of goods. At prices below P1 there will be no change in supply as that is met by domestic suppliers. At prices above P1 the (total) supply curve shifts to the right by the amount of the quota. The new equilibrium is where domestic demand is equal to total supply. The price has increased to Pq. Domestic demand will now be Q2 and domestic supply will he Q3. The shortfall is Q3-Q2 which is the amount that is imported. Imports have fallen.

Other Methods or Protectionism
1. Embargoes - bans on countries or products.
2. Depreciating the value of the currency to make home produced goods cheaper.
3. Tight regulations on production standards.
4. Subsidies to home producers.

Problems with Protectionism
1. Other countries may retaliate.
2. Trade may be diverted away from the more efficient producers.
3. Benefits from specialisation are not fully exploited.
4. Prices will tend to be higher so lower consumer surplus.
5. There may be less choice for consumers.
6. Protecting inefficient home industries is encouraging the inefficiency to continue.

Notes

Notes

Notes

Printed in Great Britain
by Amazon

12782900R00052